Short Japanese Stories For Language Learners

Grow Your Vocabulary The Fun Way!

Takumi Nonaka

Table Of Contents

Chapter 1: First Story - Sarah's Morning Rush

Early in the morning, it is 7:00 a.m. The alarm o'clock strikes on as Sarah rushes out of her bed, very refreshed and happy. Sarah says: "Good Morning!" She rushes to the kitchen to get some of the fresh pancakes that her mom was preparing earlier.

"Wait! Wash your face and hands first." Says the mother.

"Oh! Alright, I forgot about that." Reply's Sarah as she rushes back to the restroom to wash her face and hands, then brushes her teeth and gets ready for having breakfast.

"Alright! I think I am ready by now." Says Sarah and goes back to the kitchen where her mother, father and little brother were gathered to have breakfast together.

Meanwhile, they gathered around the kitchen table, as the smell of the freshly baked pancakes was irresistible. They all have pancakes with different toppings. Some like chocolate, peanut butter, maple syrup and strawberries.

Sarah loves those freshly baked pancakes that her mother makes every morning. She cannot start her day without a healthy, tasty breakfast with her family. After they finished all their breakfast, Sarah would help her mother quickly clean the dishes and then rushes back to get her backpack and head to school.

"Now I am ready to start my day and study hard!" Says Sarah. Then, she kisses her mom and dad and then gets on the school bus, excited about the classes and learning.

第1話: サラのラッシュモーニング

　　早朝7時、目覚まし時計が鳴り、サラはベッドから飛び出し、とても爽やかで幸せそうだ。サラは「おはようございます！」と言った。　彼女はキッチンに駆け込み、お母さんがさっきから準備していた焼きたてのパンケーキを取りに行った。

　　「待て！まずは、顔と手を洗ってね」　母親が言った。

　　「あ！そうか、忘れてちゃったごめんね！」　サラが返事した。そして、急いでトイレに戻り、顔と手を洗い、歯を磨き、朝食をとる準備をした。

　　「よし！そろそろ準備ができたようだ」　サラはそう言って、母と父と弟が集まって朝食をとっているキッチンへ戻っていきた。

　　一方、焼きたてパンケーキの香りがたまらない彼らは、キッチンのテーブルを囲んでいた。みんなそれぞれ違うトッピングをしたパンケーキを食べる。チョコレートやピーナツバター、メープルシロップ、イチゴが好きな人もいる。

　　サラは、母親が毎朝作ってくれる焼きたてのパンケーキが大好きだ。健康的でおいしい朝食を家族と一緒に食べないと、一日が始まらないのだ。　朝食を食べ終わると、サラは母親を手伝って皿洗いをし、急いでバックパックを取って学校へ向かって。

「これで、一日の始まりと勉強を頑張る準備ができました！」と、サラは言った。そして、お父さんとお母さんにキスをして、これから始まる授業と勉強に胸を躍らせながら、スクールバスに乗り込んだ。

1. Vocabulary List: 第 1 話単語リスト：

英語	日本語
Rush	ラッシュ
Alarm O'clock	目覚まし時計
Strikes	鳴り
Freshly Backed	焼きたて
I forgot about that	そうか、忘れた
Meanwhile	一方
Topping	トッピング
Healthy	健康的
Chocolate	チョコレート
Peanut Butter	ピーナツバター
Maple Syrup	メープルシロップ
Strawberries	イチゴ
Help	手伝って
Clean the dishes	皿洗い
Backpack	バックパック
Irresistible	たまらない
Gathered	集まって
Head to/go to	向かって
Study hard	頑張る
Get on the bus	バスに乗る
Excited for	胸を躍らせる
Head to/go to	向かって
Excited (dancing out of excitment)	胸を躍らせながら

Chapter 2: Second Story - Fumihiro's Journey to the Zoo

On Sunday afternoon, Fumihiro prepares for his first adventure. He was going to visit the local Zoo in the small town where he lived. Since Primary school, Fumihiro had always liked going to the Zoo. He would enjoy spending the time in nature and watching the wildest animals behind the cages.

"Why do we always have to keep the animals in the Zoo in cages? And pets are held with leashes around their necks?" Fumihiro thought to himself.

Although, his favourite part was visiting the Antarctica animals show because he liked the penguins and thought they looked funny when they were walking together. And the seals swimming altogether. Unfortunately, the Antarctic animals section of the Zoo was closed during the summer for reconstruction works.

Fumihiro visited the next section in the Zoo, the wild cats. The Tsushima leopard cat, with its long tail, fluffy fur, and massive body triple the size of a pet cat. Fumihiro got closer to having a better look. The wild cat was looking up the ceiling and going around in circles. The cat looked lost within the cage. In other words, it was looking for an escape from there, to go back again to the wildlife.

"Could this cat be unhappy there behind the glass? It looked like the wild cat had everything they would need, food, shelter, a swing, and natural trees. But there still seems one thing that is bothering the cat that it does not feel at home." - Fumihiro thought to himself again.

Fumihiro looked around and saw one of the zoo guards, so he went straight to ask them what he was thinking about.

"Hello! I have a question. Would you mind me asking, sir?" Said Fumihiro.

"Hello, young fella! Yes, please do ask me anything." Replied the guard.

"Why does the wild cat looks worried about something there?" Said Fumihiro.

"Worried? What do you mean?" Said the guard

"I think that cat wants to find a way outside the cage, I was watching it for a while, and it seemed uncomfortable there. Have you noticed something like that before?" Said Fumihiro in wonder.

"Oh, right! Do you mean that it looked furious? I think that is normal and happens to all the cats after eating; they just want to play around, you know." Said the zoo guard.

"Okay, I see! Thank you very much." Said Fumihiro and returned to see other animals in the Zoo. However, he was not yet convinced with the answer entirely. So he visited the different sections and then went back home.

Back at home, Fumihiro's mother had already prepared dinner. She was waiting for him to get back so they would eat together. His mother had prepared some pasta. At the dinner table, she asked Fumihiro, "So how was your day at the zoo, Fumihiro-Kun"?

"I had so much fun! I have seen many wild animals and spoke to the zoo guard too!" Said Fumihiro.

"That sounds brilliant! What did you talk about?" Said the mother.

"Well, I have asked him about the wild cats and why they did look furious behind the cage. He answered my questions, but I am still not sure about that." Said Fumihiro.

"And what did he say to you?" Asked his mother curiously.

"He said that most cats are like that. They want to play around after they eat. But I still think that there was another reason for that." said Fumihiro.

"Such a smart question to ask Fumihiro. I think that you are right; even though wild animals have food and all the luxury they would want, they are still missing one thing." Said his mother.

"What is that one thing?" Asked Fumihiro.

"It's their feeling of freedom." Replied his mother.

"You are right; they cannot be free behind the cage. I hope that one day they would have that freedom." Said Fumihiro.

"I hope so, I hope so, my darling Fumihiro." Replied his mother.

第2話: ふみひろくん動物園の旅

　日曜日の午後、ふみひろくんは初めての冒険の準備をする。小さな町にある動物園に行くことになったのだ。ふみひろくんは小学生の頃から動物園に行くのが好きだった。自然の中で過ごし、檻の中にいる野生の動物たちを見るのが楽しみだったのだ。

「なぜ、いつも動物園の動物は檻の中にいるのだろう？そして、ペットは首に鎖でつながれているのか？」　ふみひろくんがそう思っていた。

ペンギンが好きで、一緒歩いている姿が面白いと思ったからそうだった。そして、アザラシが一緒に泳いでいる姿も好きなようだ。　残念ながら、夏の期間中に動物園の南
極セクションは改築工事のため閉鎖されてきたそうだ。

ふみひろくんは動物園の次のコーナー、野生の猫たちを訪ねた。ツシマヤマネコは、長い尾とふわふわの毛、そして愛猫の3倍の大きさの巨体を持つ。ふみひろくんはもっとよく見ようと近づいた。野生の猫は、天井を見上げながら、ぐるぐると回っている。檻の中で迷っているようだ。つまり、そこから脱出して、また野生の世界に戻ろうとしているのだ。

「この猫はガラスの向こうで不幸になっているのだろうか？餌、泊めるところ、ブランコ、自然の木々など、野良猫に必要なものはすべて揃っているように見えました。しかし、まだひとつだけ、猫がくつろげないことがあるようだ。」 ― ふみひろくんは改めてそう思った。

　　ふみひろくんは周りを見渡すと、動物園の警備員が一人いたので、そのまま何を考えているのか聞きに行った。

「こんにちは！質問があります。お伺いしてもよろしいでしょうか。」 とふみひろくんが聞きた。

「こんにちは 少年よ はい、何でも聞いてください！」と警備員は答えた。

「なぜ、野良猫はそこで何かを心配しているように見えるのでしょうか。」とふみひろくんが言いた。

「心配するのか。どういう意味でしょうか」— 警備員が言った。

「あの猫はケージの外に出たいんだと思うんだ。しばらく見ていたんだが、どうも居心地が悪いそうで。前にそういうことに気づいたことがあったのか」ふみひろくんは不思議そうに言った。

「ああ、そうか！激怒しているように見えたということでしょうか。それは普通のことで、どの猫も食後は遊びたいだけだと思ってよ」 と動物園の警備員が言った。

家に帰ると、ふみひろくんの母親がすでに夕食の支度をしていた。一緒に食べようと、ふみひろくんが帰ってくるのを待っていたのだ。母親はパスタを用意していた。夕食の席で、お母さんはふみひろくんに、「ふみひろくん、動物園はどうだった？」とお母さんが聞きた。

「とても楽しかっただよ！たくさんの野生動物を見たし、動物園の警備員さんにも話しかけたよ！」 とふみひろくんが言った。

「素晴らしいだよね！ 何を話していたんのか」と母親は言いた。「さて、私は野良猫について、なぜ檻の向こうで猛烈な顔をしていたのか、聞きたことがあった。警備員さんは僕の質問に答えたが、僕はまだそれについて確信が持てない」とふみひろくんが言った。

「それで彼は何て言ったの」母親は不思議そうに聞かれた。

「ほとんどの猫がそうだと言っていました。ご飯を食べたら遊びたくなるんだって。でも、もうひとつ理由があると思うんだよね」とふみひろくんが言いた。

「それは、とてもかしこい質問だね！野生動物には食べ物も贅沢な生活もあるのに、ひとつだけ足りないものがあるのだ」とお母さんは言った。

「あれってなんだろうか」　とふみひろくんは聞かれた。

「それは彼らの自由な気持ちだ。」お母さんはそう答えた。

「そのとおり、檻の中では自由にはなれない。いつか自由を手に入れられるといいんだけどね」とふみひろくんが言いた。

「そうだといいわね、ふみひろくん！」　お母さんがそう答えた。

2. Vocabulary List: 第2話単語リスト：

英語	日本語
Cage	織
Zoo	動物園
Leash/Chain	鎖
Wild	野性
Keep	飼う
Antarctica	南極
Penguins	ペンギン
Seal	アザラシ
Unfortunately	残念ながら
Wild cat	野生の猫
Tsushima Cat	ツシマヤマネコ
Fluffy fur	ふわふわの毛
Massive Body	大きさの巨体
Going around in Circles	ぐるぐると回っている
Unhappy	不幸
Shelter	泊まるところ
Swing	ブランコ
Zoo Guard	警備員
Worried	心配する
Fella	少年
Curiously/Wonder	不思議
Luxurious Life	贅沢な生活

Chapter 3: Third Story - Lisa's Bucket List

Once, there was a very ambitious girl in her 20's, her name was Lisa. She wanted to do many things and had a great passion for adventures. Lisa was very enthusiastic. Every day she wakes up early and gets ready for a new opportunity to experience the world differently. She was what the other people called her "a dreamer."

Lisa was also a good pianist since she was 5 years old. She had been practising the piano for around 15 years, and she thinks that she wants to play it in public one day.

Even though her mother was the first person to encourage her to take piano lessons at an early age, she was less encouraging as she got very busy with her everyday work as a university professor.

First, she would wash her face and tidy up her hair to take on the day. She goes to the kitchen and pours a cup of Brazilian coffee in a mug with the capital letter (L). Then she goes to her room where there's a large windowpane and a desk.
She opens the window and takes a deep breath, inhaling some fresh air in.
"Yes, time to get some work done now." - Lisa said.

Then, she opens her notepad and gets a pencil to start writing her bucket list. As she wanted to do so many things in her life. She always wanted to go on adventures around the world. As she was pretty excited about the upcoming year, so she tried to prepare a list of her future plans and experiences.

"So, it would be a brilliant idea for me to start writing the bucket list!" - Lisa thought to herself.

She sat down and wrote down the following list:

- Go swimming in the ocean while its raining.
- Go to an all-you-can-eat hamburger restaurant.
- Travel around the world and see the seven wonders.
- Travel to Italy and visit Milan City.
- Study Architecture in Italy.
- Go to Maroon 5 live concert.
- To play the piano in public one day in front of many people.
- Go on a week-long cruise.
- Buy a house by the ocean with a small flower garden.
- Find fun and exciting words.

After she rushed and wrote all her wishes down the notebook, she was very excited for a moment that she screamed out loud. As soon as she finished writing this list, she believed that some of these wishes would come true very soon. Although she did not care what other people would think of her list, she decided to share it with Emily's best friend.

The next day, Lisa went to school while she was so excited to meet her best friend Emily and tell her about her bucket list. All the places she wanted to travel to and the things she wanted to do. Even though Emily was Lisa's best friend, she was a very jealous girl, and she usually wanted to do almost everything that Lisa does. On the other hand, Lisa did not pay attention that Emily was doing everything possible just to be like her.

"Good morning, Emily!" Lisa said as she got her notebook out of her bag. "Would you like to check out my bucket list?"

"Yes, sure I'd love to read it please," replied Emily as she seemed very happy to get to know more details about her best friend.

"Here you go. So, what do you think?" Said Lisa.

"I think it is gorgeous, Lisa! Such a brilliant idea, I never thought of writing my list of things I wanted to do before. Perhaps I will write mine as well." Commented Emily.

"Oh, yeah definitely, you could write your own list. Just pick up the things you want to do and write them on paper."

"I know that this might sound silly. But did you know? I have always wanted to travel to Italy one day. What a coincidence. You do not mind if I write it on my list too, do you?" Emily asked boldly.

"That is okay, isn't it? I mean, people might have shared hobbies or dreams. I think it's alright!" Replied Lisa.

"Brilliant! I am very excited to write my own list now." Emily said.
"And I would like to read your list when you're done," Lisa replied.
"I hope I will go to Italy before you do." Emily with a wicked smile.
"So, you will go there before I do? We will see about that." Lisa said.
        The following day, Lisa was so excited about her bucket list that she

decided to share it with her mother over breakfast.

"Mom, I've got something to show you," Lisa said.

"What is it, darling?" Lisa's mom replied.

"I have written this bucket list of things I want to accomplish and places I want to visit in my life," Lisa replied while getting her notebook.

"Oh wow, that sounds interesting, darling." Her mom replied.

"Well, there is one thing that I am concerned about," Lisa said.
"And what is that?" Her mom said.

"When I showed my list to my best friend Emily, she said that she will go first to Italy before I do," Lisa said. "And I got worried for a bit that I don't want her to go before I do; I regret sharing with her."

"Lisa, darling! You do not have to be worried. After all, life is not a competition. So, if she goes first or you do. It does not matter. As long as you work hard and make those things from your list become true." Said the mother.

"You are right!" Said Lisa. "I just need to work harder from now on."

"I think that I want to start studying Italian. That would be the first step getting closer to accomplishing my list!" She was so happy that she jumped out of her chair to hug and kiss her mom.

"That's right! You can start learning from today. Nothing is impossible." Said her mom.

"Thank you, mom!" Said Lisa.

Lisa was ready to take this challenge and work harder for her new year goals. She took up Italian language classes and started reading about architecture every day. While she got her mother's support, she was ready to make her list come true one day.

第3話:リサのバケットリスト

　昔、あるところに 20代の野心家の 女 の子がいました。名前はリサだった。彼女はいろいろなことをやってみたいと思っていて、冒険心に溢れていました。リサはとても熱心で、毎日早起きして、いつもと違う世界を体験するために、新しい機会に備えていました。周りからは 「夢追い人」と呼ばれていた。

リサは5歳の頃からピアノの腕前も良かった。15年間ピアノを練習し、いつか人前で弾きたいと考えている。

母親は、幼い頃からピアノを習うことを勧めてくれたが、大学教授としての日々の仕事に忙殺され、あまり勧めてはくれなかった。

まず、顔を洗い、髪を 整 え、一日をスタートさせる。台所へ行き、大文字の （L） のついたマグカップにブラジルコーヒーを注ぐ。そして、大きな窓ガラスと 机 がある自分の部屋に行く。彼女は窓を開け、新鮮な空気を吸い込むように深呼吸をする。

「そうだ、今から仕事をする時間だ」― とリサが言った。

そして、メモ 帳 を開いて鉛筆を手に取り、バケットリストを書き始める。彼女は人生でやりたいことがたくさんあった。世界中を冒険してみたいと思っていた。この 1年をとても楽しみにしていた彼女は、将来の計画や冒険のためのリストを作ろうと思ったのだ。

「だから私がバケットリストを書き始めるのは素晴らしいアイデアだ！」

―リサはそう思った。

彼女は腰を下ろし、次のようなリストを書き出した：

雨が降る日は海に泳ぎに行く。

  2.　ハンバーガー食べ放題のレストランに行く。

  3.　世界中を旅して七不思議を見る。

  4.　イタリアを旅行し、ミラノ市を訪れる。

  5.　イタリアで建築を勉強する。

マルーン 5 のライブに行く。

  7.　いつかたくさんの人前で、演奏会でピアノを弾くこと。

  8.　一週間のクルーズに行く。

  9.　小さな花畑のある海沿いの家を買う。

楽しくて面白い仕事を見つける。

　　　急いでノートに願い事を書き込んだ後、彼女は一瞬、大声を出してしまうほど興奮した。このリストを書き終えた瞬間、彼女はこれらの願いのいくつかはすぐにでも叶うと信じていた。他の人がどう思うかは気にしなかったが、親友のエミリーにこのリストを見せることを決めた。

翌日、リサは親友のエミリーに会い、自分のバケットリストを話すのを楽しみにしながら学校へ行く。旅行したい場所や、やってみたいことを全部。エミリーはリサの親友でありながら、とても嫉妬深く、リサがすることはほとんどすべてやりたがる子でした。一方、リサは、エミリーがリサのようになりたいと願っていることに気づかない。

「おはようございます、エミリー！」 リサはバッグからノートを取り出して言った。「私のバケットリストを読んでみたいのか」

「ええ、もちろんよ、ぜひ読んでみたいわ」とエミリーは答え、親友について
もっと詳しく知ることができてとても嬉しそうでした。

「はい、どうぞ。それで、どう思う？」リサが言った。

「とっても印象的だと思っているわ！ こんな素晴らしいアイデア、今まで
自分のやりたいことリストを書くなんて 考 え もしなかったわ。多分、 私 も
書きたいと思うよ」エミリーさんがコメントした。

「ああ、確かに自分のリストを書くことができるね。やりたいことをピック
アップして、紙に書けばいいんだからね」

「バカバカしいと思うかもしれないけど。でもね、知ってた？ 私 もいつかイ
タリアに行きたいとずっと思っていたのよ。なんて偶然なんでしょう。 私 の
リストに書いてもいいんでしょうね？」エミリーは思い切って聞いてみた。

「いいんじゃない？趣味や夢は人それぞれでしょう？大丈夫だと思う！」 リ
サが答えた。

「素晴らしい! 今から自分のリストを書くのはとても楽しみ」とエミリーが言
った。

「そして、あなたが書き終えたら、あなたのリストを読んでみたいわ」 リサ
が答えた。

「　　　　　　　　　　　　　　　　　　　　　　　　　　　　　私
はあなたより先にイタリアに行きたいわ」邪悪な笑みを浮かべたエミリー。

「じゃあ、私 より先にイタリアに行くのね？まあ、様子を見てみよう」リサ
が言った。

　　翌朝、リサは自分のバケットリストに興奮し、 朝 食 の席で母親にそれ
を披露することにした。

「ママ、見せたいものがあるの」リサはそう言いた。

「何かしら？」 リサのお母さんは答えた。

「 私 は人生で成し遂げたいことや行きたい場所を書いたバケットリストを作ったの」 リサはノートを手に取りながら答えた。

「わあ、面白そうね、リちゃん」 リサの母親が答えた。

「まあ、ひとつだけ気になることがあるんだけどね」 とリサが返事した。

「それは何？」 とお母さんが聞きた。

「親友エミリーに 私 のリストを見せたら、 私 より先にイタリアに行くと言われた。そして、私 は彼女に先に行かれては困ると少し心配になり、彼女と共有したことを後悔したね」 とリサが言った。

「リサ、ダーリン！そういう事心配する必要がないね。結局のところ、人生は競争ではない。だから、彼女が先に行くか、あなたが先に行くか。それは本当に重要なことではないと思う。あなたが一生懸命頑張ってて、リストにあることを実現しさえすれば良いね」と母親は言いた。

「その通りだ！」 リサが言った。「これからもっと頑張ればいいんだ」

「イタリア語の勉強を始めようと思うの。それがリストの達成に近づく第一歩になるわ!」 リサはとても喜んで、椅子から飛び降りてお母さんに抱きつき、キスをした。

「その通りだよね! 今日から学んで。不可能なことはないんだ」 とお母さんが言いた。

「ありがとう、ママ！」 リサがそう言いた。

　それで、リサはこの挑戦を受け止め、新年の目標に向かってより一層努力する覚悟を決めた。リサはイタリア語のクラスを取り、毎日建築に関する本を読むようになりました。母親のサポートを受けながら、彼女はいつか自分のリストを実現させようと思っていた。

第3話単語リスト：3. Vocabulary List:

英語	日本語
Bucket List	バケットリスト
Ambitious Person	野心家
Adventurous / Passionate Adventurer	冒険心
Enthusiastic	熱心
a dreamer	夢追い人
To Play in public	人の前を弾く
Encouraged	勧めてくれた
tidy up her hair	髪を整え
Pour	注ぐ
capital letter	大きな文字
windowpane	窓ガラス
Fresh Air	新鮮な空気
Get some work done	仕事をする時間
Brilliant idea	素晴らしいアイデア
all-you-can-eat	食べ放題
seven wonders	七不思議
Architecture	建築
in front of many people	たくさんの人前で
flower garden	花畑
Decided	決めた
Best Friend	親友
Jealousy / Envy	嫉妬
Utmost effort	一生懸命
Implementation	実現

Chapter 4: Fourth Story - The Lucky Mandarine

In January, I was living in Tokushima Prefecture, Japan, and craving some fruits. So, I went downtown to the market and bought a big fruit basket, it was the local mandarin oranges. Which is the orange tiny little fruit that, once you peel it, would be very soft and sweet from the inside. It was still entirely freezing in the city, and the news forecasted that it would snow tomorrow. So, I finished shopping while it was freezing outside and went back to my room.

I have got the fruits that I have been craving for some time. I was wondering what my roommates would say about that surprise. They also liked fruits so much, but they would instead buy something else since they were expensive.

Yukihiro would always tell me: "I'd rather spend my money or more fancy food and filling, like real food perhaps or meat."

"But fruits are more nutritious than all the junk food you like." And that would be my usual comment.

However, Yukihiro had moved out a month ago and went back to living with his grandparents in Tokyo prefecture. So, we have not met since then. The apartment seemed less lively than it used to be, without that noisy Yukihiro, I thought. The house cat jumped on the top of the fridge as I opened the rusty fridge door to put the fruits and veggies that I had brought earlier. My cat started staring at me while purring instantly and moving its tail around clockwise. I got some cold fresh milk out of the fridge and poured it into the cats' plate marked with "Chibi-chan." As Chibi started licking the milk as fast as I reached the ground where I placed the container on the side.

"You're a good cat, Chibi. You must have been hungry." - I said to the cat. Then I started watching the news again on that tiny little TV screen to get some distraction. The breaking news noted that the snowstorm would come tomorrow, and it will be one of the most prolonged storms since the 1980s.

"The weather forecast for tomorrow expects to cover the entire Shikoku Island of Japan with over 10 meters of snow. It is also

advised to avoid using transportation as possible." - Said the news reporter on the NHK television.

I was surprised by the news, but I did not freak out at all. I do not mind being stuck inside the house for a couple of days. Perhaps I would be able to finish working on my painting project. So, I got the brush and my painting tools, and I sat down for a moment to set the table near my window.

It started to rain, and I saw many people holding very colourful umbrellas from my window in the streets. So, I thought of Exceptional painting. Perhaps the mixture of umbrellas with the snow's colours was so bright, and I will make the purity of snow even more attractive. So, I begin drawing very focused on every brush movement while keeping my eye on the window, witnessing the streets in silence.

Then again, to break the silence, I turned on the radio to listen to some classical music. It was Tokushima's local radio broadcast. *"The Nutcracker (Suite) Op. 71a"* by the composer Tchaikovsky played on.

I was a little bit hungry, so I went to the fridge and opened the drawer where I had put the fruits earlier to grab a piece of Mandarine orange. The cat was staring at me with a surprised look that I interpreted as:

"What are you doing, mate?!"

"I am hungry; you had your milk, didn't you?" - I replied to the silent cat as it raised its whiskers with a careless look.

"Alright! I don't think you'd like some oranges, do you? I've read an article in the daily newspaper that cats don't like citrus fruits anyway."

As I got the Mandarine orange, a small white tape was attached to it. I removed the white tape to find out it has some old Kanji writing (Dai-an). Which translates to 'Lucky Day' I smiled at the cat purring in the corner and had the delicious Mandarine while feeling relieved that soon, the storm will pass too.

第４話：大安のみかん

　1月、私は徳島県に住んでいたのですが、どうしてもフルーツが食べたくなりた。そこで、街の市場に行き、大きな果物かごを買いた。それは地元のみかんだった。オレンジ色の小さな果物で、皮をむくと中からとても柔らかくて甘いものが出てくる。街はまだとても寒く、ニュースでは明日は雪が降るという予報が出ていた。そんなわけで、外が寒い中買い物を済ませ、部屋に戻りた。

いつか食べたいと思っていたフルーツを手に入れた。このサプライズをルームメイトはどう思うだろうかと考えていた。彼らもフルーツは大好きなのですが、高いので他のものを買おうと思っていたのだ。

ゆきひろはいつも、「俺はお金を使うなら、もっと豪華な食べ物や食べ応えのあるもの、例えば本物の食べ物やお肉がいい」と言うのだ。

「でも、君の好きなジャンクフードより、果物の方が栄養価が高いよ」。というのが、私のいつものコメントだった。

　しかし、ゆきひろは1ヶ月前に家を引っ越したから、東京都の祖父母の家に戻っていた。だから、それ以来、会っていない。あの騒がしいゆきひろがいないアパートは、以前より活気がないように思えた。さっき持ってきた野菜や果物を入れようと錆びた冷蔵庫の扉を開けると、家の猫が冷蔵庫の上に飛び乗った。家猫は即座にゴロゴロしながら私を見つめ始め、尻尾を時計回りに動かしている。私は冷蔵庫から冷たい牛乳を取り出し、「チビちゃん」の書かれた猫の皿に注いだ。チビちゃんは、私がお皿を置いた地面に手を伸ばすと、すぐにミルクを舐め始めた。

「いい猫だね、チビちゃん！お腹が空いていたんだろう」—と、猫に言いた。

それから 私 は気晴らしにあの小さなテレビ画面で再びニュースを見始めた。
速報では、明日から吹雪になり、1980年代以降で最も長い吹雪になることだった。

「明日の天気予報では、四国全域で 10 メートルを超える積雪が予想されています。または、交通機関の利用はできるだけ控えるようにことお願いいたします」 —と NHK テレビのニュースレポーターが言った。

このニュースには驚いたなのに、まったく動じゃなかった。2～3日頃で家の中に閉じこもっていても平気だと思った。もしかしたら、絵の制作ができるかもしれない。そこで、筆と絵の道具を持って、窓際のテーブルにちょっと腰掛けてみた。

　雨が降り出し、窓から見えた街角では、たくさんの人々が色とりどりの傘をさしているのが見えた。そこで僕は、特別な絵画について思いつきた。おそらく、傘と雪が混ざり合い、色彩はとても鮮やかで、雪の純度はより魅力的なものになるはずだ。そこで僕は、窓から目を離せず、静かに通りを見ながら、筆の動きひとつひとつに集 中して描き始めた。

そしてまた、沈黙を破るために、ラジオをつけてクラシック音楽を聴いた。徳島ローカルラジオの放送だった。作曲家チャイコフスキーの「くるみ割り人形（組曲）作曲品 71A」が流れた。少しお 腹 が空いたので、冷蔵庫に行き、さっき果物を入れておいた引き出しを開けて、マンダリンオレンジを一個手に取った。猫は、僕が解釈したとおりの驚いた顔で僕を見つめていた。

「お前！何してるんだ？」

「お腹が空いたわ。 先にミルクを飲んだでしょ？」— 無言の猫が油断した様子でヒゲを上げながら、僕はそう答えた。

「まあ！みかんは嫌いかな？猫は柑橘類が嫌いだって、毎日新聞の記事で読んだことがあるんだよね～」。

　みかんを手にすると、小さな白いテープが貼られていた。白いテープを剥がしてみると、そこには「大安」古い漢字で書いてあった。隅でゴロゴロしている猫に微笑みながら、もうすぐ嵐も過ぎ去るという安心の気持ちで美味しいみかんをいただいた。

4. Vocabulary List: 単４語リスト：

英語	日本語
Tokushima Prefecture	徳島県
Food Craving / Craving to eat	食べたくなりた
Mandarin	みかん
Forecast	予報
I have got the fruits	フルーツを手に入れた
Fancy food	豪華な食べ物
Nutritious	栄養価が高い
Junk food	ジャンクフード
Moved out	引っ越た
Grandparents	祖父母
Less lively	活気がない
Rusty fridge	錆った冷蔵庫
Veggies / Vegetables	野菜
Purring (sound e.g., for cats)	ゴロゴロ
Tail (of an animal)	尻尾
Clockwise	時計回り
Poured	注いだ
Ground / Earth surface	地面
Must be Hungry	お腹が空いていた
Citrus fruits	柑橘類
Calmness / coolness	平気
Surprised	驚いた
Purity (of a substance)	純度
Charming	魅力的
To smile	微笑み
Recreation	気晴らし

Chapter 5: Fifth Story - Tokyo's Merry Christmas

On December 24, Christmas Eve, the sky of Tokyo City was lighted up with colourful illuminations. Mia and Sasha, the two high school students, walked around the Tokyo Station. The building lights were shining as people worked in their offices for long hours overtime. And the trees were surrounded with ornaments and tiny lamps that played along with a piece of upbeat music that followed the lights simultaneously.

That night the city was crowded with many people who wanted to celebrate and walk around watching the illuminations. It was unusual due to the overwhelming number of couples around the Christmas trees and lights. Even though it was pretty crowded, the vibes were relatively peaceful. The night was cold, and most people were prepared for the cold weather. The pastry shops were overcrowded too. People were standing in lines waiting to get that white spongy Christmas cake. There was another line of people on the other side of the station. However, this time, they were waiting to buy some fried chicken before it sold out. But Sasha thought that it was a rather strange way to celebrate Christmas.

"Why do they do this every year? I grew up in the United Kingdom, and we never had such traditions." Said Sasha while he gave Mia some strange looks.

"I know what you are thinking; that must be weird a first."
"Well, I am just surprised by the traditions. Here is a little bit different from what I am used to."

"Sasha! Are you homesick already?" Mia asked.

"Homesick? Me? That cannot be." Sasha laughed.

"Well, you're just looking strange. I hope you're not homesick."

"That would be the last thing on my mind right now, trust me."

"Then what were you thinking about?" Asked Mia curiously.
"I was just wondering how the celebration took a different custom in Japan, that's all." Said Sasha.

"Well, you are completely right! I've never been abroad, but I guess it is different in every place." Commented Mia.

They both kept walking around the city, talking and laughing for hours during the night. The city never looked dark in the first place, the sky was very blue in Tokyo, and the Christmas illuminations are usually bright at night.

"I want to have ice cream! Let's eat ice cream." Shouted Mia.
"Yeah? You'd like ice cream now even though it is freezing now?"
"Yes, let's have ice cream! Common, don't be worried. It's not cold."
"Well, I'm not worried. But it's very chilling outside. You may catch a cold or something."

"No, I want an ice cream now!" Said Mia like a five-year-old child.
"Okay, let's go to that convenience store and get you something," replied Sasha.

"Yay! I am happy!" Responded Mia.

"Don't catch a cold. I don't want to be blamed for it, okay?"
"Yes, don't worry. I always have ice cream even when it's raining."

"Ice cream with rain? Are you insane?" Sasha looked very shocked.

"Yes, my mom let me eat ice cream any time of the year. So, my immune system is pretty much strong." Commented Mia.

"Well, let's see how it goes then. I am not responsible if you get sick or anything!" Said Sasha as they both entered the store.

"Welcome! How about a fried chicken for Christmas?" Asked the employee with a big smile on his face.

"We have Christmas Cake for a special offer today!" Said the owner of the store as she was very kind and welcoming.

"Thank you for your nice offer, but we are looking for something else." Said Sasha politely.

"It's over there! Over there!" Screamed Mia with excitement.
"Oh great! You've got the skills to spot the ice cream aisle very quick too." Said Sasha as they both broke in laughter.

"Yes, I told you ice cream is my profession." Said Mia.

"Did you find what you're looking for?" Sasha said.

"Oh, it's over there! And it's the last one!" Said while getting the last piece instantly.

"Yeah! You must be lucky then." Said Sasha with a smile.

It was frozen outside as they both went to a nearby park, sat on the bench and shared that soft cream.

"Here, try it. You won't regret this, I promise." Said Mia.

"Yummy! Indeed, I don't feel that much cold now." Said Sasha with a mocking look on his face.

"Totally, but the magic of the ice cream doesn't work like that. You should immerse yourself with the ice cream!" Said Mia acting as if she was the ice cream expert.

"Well, I do see your point. Once your body is cold inside, you no longer feel the freezing temperature, that's for sure. Perhaps your body absorbs the coldness of the ice cream. Then your temperature cools down to become somewhat equal to the outside temperature." Said Sasha trying to explain the theory behind Mia's love for eating ice cream during the cold winter.

"You're right, Professor Sasha." Said Mia as they both burst into laughter.

"I am not a professor. That's just common sense. Anyhow, I have some good news to tell you." Said Sasha.

Mia looked to Sasha's face, took a pause from licking the ice cream and was ready to hear what he got to say. However, Sasha hesitated for a moment.

"What is it you want to say?" Asked Mia.

"I have got excellent news, but..."
"But what? Tell me!"

"I have got accepted in Osaka University. I will be going there to study Human Sciences."

"Are you kidding me? That is wonderful news. I am happy for you." Replied Mia.

"There's only one thing that I will move out to Osaka next week."

"I will miss you so much, Sasha." Said Mia as the fireworks lit up the night sky, and the bells rang in celebration of the new year.

第5話：東京のメリークリスマス

12月24日で、東京のクリスマスイブの空は明るい色のイルミネーションで彩られていた。高校生二人のミアとサーシャは、東京駅前の町中で歩いていた。長時間残業するのオフィスで働く人たちのために、ビルの明かりが過ぎていた。そして、木々の周りにはオーナメントや小さなランプが飾られ、その 光 と同時に明るい音楽が流れていた。

その夜、街はイルミネーションを見ながら歩き、お祝いをしようとする多くの人々で賑わっていた。クリスマスツリーやイルミネーションの周りには、圧倒的な数のカップルがいて、異様な雰囲気だった。かなり混雑していても、雰囲気は比較的穏やかだった。夜は寒かったので、ほとんどの人が防寒対策をしていた。パティシエ屋も混雑していた。白いスポンジのようなクリスマスケーキを手に入れるために、人々が列を作って待っていた。駅の反対側にも人の列ができていた。しかし、今度はフライドチキンが売り切れる前に買おうと待っているのだ。しかし、サーシャは、これはちょっと奇妙なクリスマスの祝い方だと思った。

「なぜ、毎年こんなことをするのだろう？私はイギリスで育ったけど、こんな伝統的なものはなかったよ」。サーシャはそう言いながら、ミアに不思議そうな顔をした。

「何を考えているかわかるよ、初めてで変だろう」

「まあ、私はただ伝統に驚いているだけです。ここは私が慣れているところとは少し違うのものだろうか。サーシャ！もうホームシックになったのか？」—とミアが聞いた。

「ホームシック？そんなことではないよー」サーシャは笑った。

「まあ、変な顔してるだけよ。ホームシックになってないといいんだけど……」

「今はそんなこと考えることではないわよ」。

「じゃあ、何を考えていたんだ？」―ミアは不思議そうに尋ねた。

「日本ではお祝いの習慣がどう違うのかなって思っただけ」―とサーシャは言った。

「そう、その通り。私は海外に行ったことがないのですが、やはり地域によって違うのだよね」―とミアはコメントした。

二人は夜の街を歩き続け、何時間も話し、笑い続けた。そもそも街が暗く見えることはなく、東京の空はとても青いし、クリスマスのイルミネーションは夜でも明るいのが普通だ。

「アイスクリームが食べたい！ アイスクリームを食べよう」―ミアが叫んだ。

「そう？今、寒いのにアイスクリームが食べたい？」

「そうだ、アイスクリームを食べよう！ほんとに？心配しないで。寒くないよ」

「まあ、心配はしていないよ。でも、外はとても冷えるよ。風邪をひいたりしないか」。

「いやだ、今すぐアイスクリームが食べたい！」―まるで5歳の子供のようにミアは言った。

「じゃあ、コンビニで買ってこよう」サーシャが答えた。

「やったー！うれしい！」ミアはそう答えた。

「風邪をひかないようにね。責められるのは嫌 だからさ」

「はい、心配しないで。雨の日でもアイスを食べられるからね」

「雨の日にもアイスクリーム？正気か？」―サーシャはとてもショックを受けた様子した。

「そうよ、私のお母さんは一年中いつでもアイスクリームを食べ
させてくれたわ。だから、私の免疫力はかなり高いだからね」―
とミアがコメントした。

「さて、どうなることやら。病気になったりしても、私は責任取
らないからよ！」―
とサーシャが言う時、二人が店内に入った。「いらっしゃいませ。
クリスマスにフライドチキンはいかがです
か？」満面の笑みで従業員に尋ねられた。

「今日は特別にクリスマスケーキを用意した、いかがでしょう
か！」と、店主はとても親切に迎えてくれた。

「ありがとうございます、でも他のものを探しているんです」サー
シャは丁寧にそう言った。

「あそこにあるよ。あそこだよ！」―ミアが興奮気味に叫びました
。

「すごい！アイスクリーム売り場もすぐに見つけることができるん
だね。とサーシャが言ったと、二人は笑い声を上げた。

「そうだ、アイスクリームは私の職業だと言っただろう」―と
ミアは言った。

「探しているものは見つかりましたか？」とサーシャが言った。

「あ、あそこです！そして最後の一個だ！」と言いながら、最後の
一枚を瞬時に手に入れた。

「そうだ！じゃあ、ラッキーなんだね」
サーシャは笑顔でそう言った。

二人は近くの公園に行き、ベンチに座ってそのソフトクリームを
分け合って食べると、外は凍っていた。

「ほら、食べてみて。後悔はさせないよ、約束するよ」―とミアは
言った。

「おいしい　確かに、今はそんなに寒さを感じないわ」サーシャは
嘲笑うような顔でそう言った。

「でも、アイスクリームの魔法はそんなものではない。アイスの中
に身を浸すといいんだよ」―とミアはまるでアイスクリームの
専門家であるかのような口ぶりで言った。

「まあ、言いたいことはわかるよ。体の中が冷えてしまえば、
凍えるような温度は感じなくなるのは確かだ。おそらく、アイスク
リームの冷たさを　体　が　吸　収　しているのでしょう。そうすると、
体温が冷えて外気温と同じくらいになるんだよー」サーシャは、
美沙が寒い冬にアイスを食べるのが好きな理由を説明したように。

「その通りだよね、サーシャ先生！」　とミアが言うと、二人は大声
で笑っていた。

「私は先生ではないよー。そんなの常識よ。とにかく、いい
知らせがあるんだ。」　とサーシャは言った。

美沙はサーシャの顔を見て、アイスクリームを舐めるのをやめ、彼
の話を聞こうとした。しかし、サーシャは少しためらった。

「言いたいことは何だ？」　とミアは尋ねた。

「素晴らしい知らせがあるのんだけど...」

「しかし、何？教えてよ！」

「大阪大学に合格した大阪大学で人間科学を勉強することになりま
した。

「冗談でしょう？それは本当にすばらしいニュースだ。嬉しい
わ！」ミアはそう答えた。

「ただ一つ、来週から大阪に引っ越するからね。」

「サーシャ！寂しくなるわー」　夜空に花火が上がり、新年を祝う鐘
がなりひびく中、ミアはそう言った。

5. Vocabulary List: 単５語リスト：

英語	日本語
Christmas Eve (Night of 24th)	クリスマスイブ
Long Overtime	長時間残業
Elimination	イルミネーション
Ornaments (Decorations)	オーナメント
Celebration	お祝い
Crowded Place	賑わっていた
Overcrowded	かなり混雑
Couples	カップル
Atmosphere	雰囲気
Almost	ほとんど
Pastry Shop	パティシエ屋
Opposite Side	反対側
Fried Chicken	フライドチキン
Different in every place	地球によって違う
Convenience Store	コンビニ
Immunity	免疫力
Blamed (Accused of something)	責められる
Profession (Specialty)	専門職
Laugh out loud	大声で笑っていた
Inside the Store	店内
Magic	魔法
Information	お知らせ
Human Science	人間科学
Joke	冗談

Chapter 6: Sixth Story - The Three Heroes of Peace

On a Spring chilling day in March, the 19 years-old freshman Ana was looking for a new adventure around the university campus. She was a very cheerful girl with steady steps as she walked. And with a proud head, Ana would stare at the sky, fearless. As she walked around the campus, she found a new pathway within the woods that she had never seen before. Then, Ana was very curious about that place. She thought that she would get there and just take a quick look. Perhaps a new adventure would be waiting for Ana.

No harm in one quick look." She thought.

As she entered the woods, there were trees; Pines, Ponderosa, and Giant Sequoia were all around her. She kept walking on steadily while wishing to unravel the mystery of the forest. She was able to hear the birds chirping on the top of trees, the waterfalls that echoed far away, and the howling wind that blew the fallen leaves away. Ana continued to walk around the forest in surprise. As if she has never seen such a forest before. The sun was shining clear on her face whenever she passed through the empty tree branches that were yet to bloom. Three trees stood there firmly as they were staring back at her face. She stepped forward to take a closer look. And noted some written letters on the big old tree:

A gift of life from the generous Professor of P...."
The rest of the letters had decayed already. Who could this professor be?" Ana was surprised, she thought.

Then she moved to the second tree and saw another mysterious hint. Indeed, the second tree as well had something written on it! Ana was astonished by that and rushed closer to try and read what was written there.

Try to find P.."

Hence, again the words were wiped out and difficult to read. Ana could not comprehend the whole meaning.

Perhaps it could have been wiped out by rain." She thought again. As Ana found herself in the middle of the three trees group, she took a step closer to the third tree to see what could be written on it.

But when she got close, there was nothing written on the third tree, she saw nothing but an old wood board with a fragment of numbers on it. The registered numbers were: (1, 22, 44, 46, 11).

Then Ana had thought about what those numbers that could actually mean. Could this be a coded message somehow on the trees?" She thought to herself.

Ana thought that this could be just her own analysis, and it could be nothing related between those trees and the forest.

Just then, she had heard a distant sweet sound of a water creek. She turned around towards where the sound was coming from. She thought of going after that sound; perhaps she may find a water stream nearby.

Then Ana walked for a long time; she did not realize it. When she was up the hill, there were many stones. As she got closer to what was there, she saw a vast sculpture standing there. The statue was of a wild deer standing up and staring at the sky. Below it there, she read the following words:

Here, and here only I could enjoy the eternal Peace."
—A memorial for the three scientist heroes who did their best in research work.

At the end of her mysterious journey, Ana was very touched by what she saw. She realized that the missing word was P = Peace", which made her think more about the world.

How amazing our nature is?" Ana said as the sunlight shined from between the tree branches down on her soft skin. And as she looked up the sky and smiled for a blessing of a new experience ahead.

第6話：平和の三勇士

　　3月のある春の日、19歳の新入生アナは、大学のキャンパスで新しい冒険をしようとしていた。彼女はとても元気で、しっかりとした足取りで歩いている。そして、誇らしげな頭で、空を見つめて、恐れを知らない。キャンパス内を歩いていると、森の中に今まで見たこともないような小道を発見した。すると、アナはその場所にとても興味を持ちました。そして、その場所に行って、ちょっとだけ見てみようと思った。もしかしたら、新しい冒険がアナを待っているかもしれない。

「ちょっと見てみるだけなら害はない」　彼女はそう思った。

　森に入ると、松やポンデローサ、ジャイアント・セコイアなどの木々が周囲に広がっていた。この森の謎を解き明かしたい、と思いながら、彼女はひたすら歩き続けた。木々の上でさえずる鳥の声、遠くで響く滝の音、落ち葉を吹き飛ばす風の音……。アナは驚きながら森を歩き続けた。こんな森は見たことがない、と。まだ花の咲いていない空っぽの枝を通るたびに、太陽の光が彼女の顔にはっきりと射してくる。3　　本の木がしっかりと立っていて、彼女の顔を見つめている。彼女は一歩前に出て、よく見てみた。すると、大きな木に文字が書かれているのに気づいた。

　　　「寛大な教授からの生命の贈り物はP……」。
残りの文字はすでに朽ち果てていた。

「この教授は誰なんだろう？」―アナは驚いた。

そして、2本目の木に目を移すと、これまた不思議なヒントがあった。確かに、2本目の木にも何かが書かれていたのだ。アナは驚いて、急いで近づいて、そこに書いてあることを読もうとした。

「P...を探してみてください」

しかし、またしても文字が消えていて、読みにくい。アナには、その意味がよくわからなかった。

「もしかしたら、雨で消えてしまったのかもしれない。そう思った。

アナは、3本の木の真ん中にいることに気づき、3本目の木に何が書かれているのか確認するために、一歩近づいた。

しかし、近づいてみると、3本目の木には何も書かれておらず、古い木の板に数字の断片が書かれているだけだった。登録された数字 (1, 22, 44, 46, 11).

「これは木に書かれた暗号なのだろうか？」そのときアナは、この数字が何を意味しているのか？　—とアナが考えた。

しかし、これはアナの勝手な思い込みで、木と森には何の関係もないのではと思っていた。

　　そのとき、遠くから小川の流れる音が聞こえた。アナはその音のするほうに振り向いた。その音を追って、近くに小川があるかもしれない。

　　そして、アナは気づかぬうちに長い間歩いていた。丘上に行くと、たくさんの石があった。そこに近づくと、大きな彫刻が立っているのが見えた。野生の鹿が立っていて、空を見つめている。その下には、次のような言葉が書かれていた。

　「ここでは、ここでしかないところで、私達は永遠の平和を
楽しむことができない」　研究活動に全力を尽くした三人の科学者
の勇者たちへの追悼の言葉である。

　　不思議な旅の終わりに、アナはとても感動した。そして、足り
ない言葉は　「P ＝ 平和」であることに気づき、さらに世界について
考えるようになる。

　「私達の自然はなんて素晴らしいんだろう！」木の枝の　間　から
差し込む陽光が、アナの柔らかい肌に降り注ぐと、アナが言った。
そして、空を見上げて、これから始まる新　しい体験の祝福に
微笑んだ。

6. Vocabulary List: 単6語リスト：

英語	日本語
Freshman	新入生
Pine tree	松
Ponderosa (tall timber pine trees)	ポンデローサ
Giant Sequoia (California trees)	ジャイアント・セコイア
Campus (in university)	キャンパス
Surrounding	周囲
Puzzle	謎
Fallen Leaves	落ち葉
Tree branch	えた
Tolerance	寛大
Firmly / Steady	しっかり
Professor	教授
Rust away	朽ち果て
Hard to read	読みにくい
Hill top	丘上
Carving / Engraving	彫刻
Registered	登録
To turn face around / Turn around	振り向く
Wild Deer	野生の鹿
Stare	見つめて
Eternity	永遠
Heroes	勇者
Memorial	追悼
Moved emotionally	感動
Blessing	祝福

Chapter 7: Seventh Story - The Unexpected Librarian

Once upon a time, there was a man who loved reading books. David was a man that was down to earth and easy-going throughout his life. He was obsessed with reading books and words from everything. Even the newspaper, which meant nothing to him nor his interest. He would read anything that fell underneath his hands.

In the morning, while having breakfast, he would be reading one or two books. Before bed, he would read on candlelight until he fell asleep. He fell in love with every word he read and never tired of reading. When he stops to tie his shoes in before heading outside his house, he finds a piece of newspaper on the ground. So David would spend another 10 minutes just reading it before he goes out. Then he took the one-hour train to the public library. There he felt more like himself. No distractions from anyone. Everyone is reading and writing at the same time. Like they were a family to him. He knew that he would always enjoy his time there as it is the best space for doing what he likes the most; reading.

He was looking for some books to get from the Science Fiction section at the library. He stumbled upon "The Space of a Galactic Empire", the book that first got his interest from afar. As soon as he got closer to check out that book, he saw another person interested in that book. There she was, Lexi. A beautiful young girl with curly shiny hair. Whom she was staring at the same book.

"Are you into Si-Fi books?" - David asked.

"Yes, I am! I am just interested in reading this book. Excuse me if you wanted it first, you can have it by all means." Lexi said.

"Oh, thank you! That is very generous of you," replied David.
"But, you have to give me the book anyhow first, if you are going to check it out this library."

"Do I have to? Why?" David asked in suspense.
"Well, obviously because I work here," Lexi said.

"I just want to read it here. I won't take it back home." David said.
"Well, may I get to know your name?" She asked.

David came close to Lexi and whispered: "I don't want to tell you."

"Okay, enjoy your doomed planet book then," Lexi said and moved away.
"Wait, I was just kidding. I am David, and you are?"

"Crazy David, what a funny name," Lexi said as she laughed and left. Then he smiled and thought that he would read his book. But he was distracted from his reading by her presence earlier. He wanted to say something more, but she already had left.

"Why did I stop?" He asked himself.

"I should have said something to her."

But David went back to the reading section, opened the book and started reading. He was interested in knowing more about the novel between his hands, but his mind was drifting towards other directions.

"I won't hesitate this time," David said to himself.

Then he went down to the ground floor where he saw Lexi again.

"Hey, can you at least tell me your name?" David asked.

"Lexi, my name is Lexi." She said to him.

David Smiled and felt happy that he got to know Lexi. He thought how a small act of kindness and open-mindedness could change a lot in ones' life.

第7話：思いがけない司書

　今は昔、あるところに本を読むのが大好きな男がいた。デービッドは、生涯を通じて、地に足の着いた、のんびりした男だった。彼は、何から何まで本や言葉を読むことに夢中だった。新聞には興味がなかったものが、手にしたものは何でも読んでいた。朝は、朝食をとりながら、1冊か2冊の本を読んでいた。寝る前にも、ろうそくの明かりの中で、眠くなるまで読んでいた。読書は飽きることがない。ある日、家の外に出る前に靴ひもを結ぼうとしたとき、地面に新聞紙が落ちているのを見つける。そこでデービッドは、出かける前にもう10分ほど、ただそれを読むことに費やすのであった。そして、1時間かけて電車に乗り、公立図書館に行くのである。そこで彼は、より自分らしく感じることができた。誰からも邪魔されない。みんなが同時に本を読んだり、文章を書いたりしている。彼にとっては家族のようなものだ。図書館は、自分が一番好きなこと、つまり読書をするのに最適な空間だから、そこで過ごす時間はいつも楽しいと思った。

図書館でSFのコーナーにある本を探していた。その中で、「銀河帝国の宇宙」という本を見つけた。その本を借りようと近づいた途端、その本に興味を持っている別の人を見かけた。

そこにいたのは、レキシーだった。艶やかなカール一髪をした少女は美しいだった。彼女も同じ本をじっと見ていた。

「Si-Fiの本が好きなの？」― とデービッドが聞いた。

「はい、そうです！ただ、この本に興味があるんだ。そうだよ！この本を読んでみたいなら、最初取っても良いよ！」―とレクシーは言った。

「ああ、ありがとうございます！それはとてもやさしいだよ」。

「でも、この図書館で借りるなら、まずこの本を渡してもらわないとね」

「そうしなきゃいけないの？どうして？デービッドは不安げに聞いた」。

「まあ、明らかに　私
はここで働いているからね」とレクシーは言った。

「僕はただここで読みたいだけなの。家に持って帰らないわ」。とデービッドが言った。

「さて、あなたの名前を教えてもらってもいいですか？」　と彼女は尋ねた。

デービッドはレクシーに近づき、私語した。

「言いたくないよ！」

「わかったわ、じゃあ銀河帝国宇宙の本を楽しんでね」とレキシーはそう言って離れた。

「待てよ、冗談だよ。僕はデービッド、君は？」

「クレイジー・デービッド、面白い名前わね」とレクシーは
笑いながらそう言って去っていった。

そして微笑みながら、本を読もうと思った。しかし、彼は彼女の
存在によって読書から気を取られてしまった。彼はもっと何か
言おうとしたが、彼女はすでに帰っていった。

「なぜ俺は立ち止まってしまったのか？」 彼は自分に問いかけた。

「彼女に何か言うべきだった」 しかし、デービッドは読書コーナーに戻り、本を開いて読み始めた。彼は両手の 間 にある小説についてもっと読みたいと思ったが、 心 は他の方向へ流れていた。

「今度はためらわないぞ。」― デービッドは自分に言い聞かせた。そして、1階に降りた。そこで彼は 再
びレキシーにもう一度会った。

「ねぇ、名前だけでも教えてくれない？」―
デービッドはそう聞かれた。

「レキシー、 私 の名前はレキシーだよ」―と彼女が言った。
デービッドは微笑みながら、レキシーと知り合いになれたことを
嬉しく思った。彼は、開放性と親切心 で態度が、自分の人生を
大きく変えることができるのだと思っていた。

7.Vocabulary List: 単 7 語リスト :

英語	日本語
Librarian	司書
Unexpected (person/event)	思いがけない
Interest	興味
One's lifetime	生涯
Newspaper	新聞
Candle	ろうそく
Same time	同時
Galactic Empire	銀河帝国
Space	宇宙
Science Fiction	サイエンスフィクション (SF)
Corner / Section	コーナー
Reading Corner	読書コーナー
Suitable / Appropriate	最適
Spend (Time)	費やす
Stumbled upon (Found)	見つけた
Just (now, at the moment)	途端
Shiny hair	艶やか
Curly hair	カール一髪
Both hands	両手
Kind person	やさしい
Whispered	私語
Once again	再び
Behaviour/attitude	態度
Openness (personality)	開放性 (性格)
Kindness	親切心

My final request…

Being a smaller author, reviews help me tremendously!

It would mean the world to me if you could leave a review.

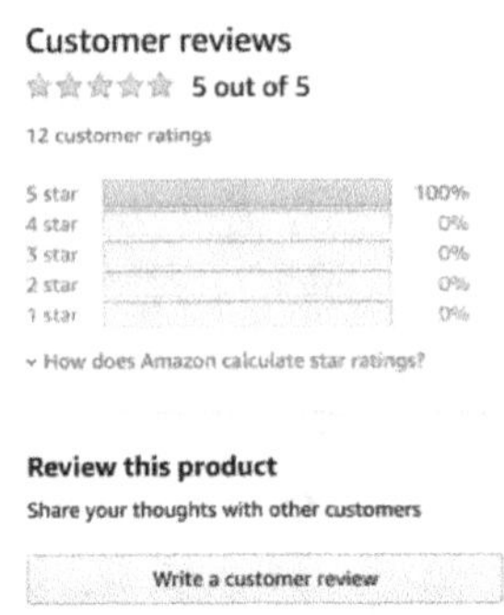

If you liked reading this book and learned a thing or two, please let me know!

It only takes 30 seconds but means so much to me!

Thank you and I can't wait to see your thought.

Conclusion

We hope that you have enjoyed this work of fictional short stories and that you were able to pick up new vocabularies that can help you in your daily conversation. This book was dedicated to reading short stories and learning about cultural and lingual aspects with an exciting language learning style. Both learners of English and Japanese can benefit from these stories and vocabulary lists.

Resources:

Bui Hoang Hai. (2012). *Meaning of みかん in Japanese* | RomajiDesu Japanese dictionary. Romajidesu.com.

徳島県 | 徳島県ホームページ. (2017). 徳島県ホームページ. https://www.pref.tokushima.lg.jp/

ツシマヤマネコについて|対馬市. (2021). Nagasaki.jp. https://www.city.tsushima.nagasaki.jp

たなぼた. (2019, August 16). Bucket list(バケットリスト)の意味とは？ 作り方のコツも解説！
　　TANAKA La BOTAMOCHI. https://tanarizm.com/whats-bucket-list

The Nutcracker (suite), Op.71a (Tchaikovsky, Pyotr) - IMSLP/ペトルッチ楽譜ライブラリー: パブリックドメインの無料楽譜. (2021). Imslp.org. https://imslp.org/wiki/The_Nutcracker_(suite),_Op.71a_(Tchaikovsky,_Pyotr)

Oishimaya Sen Nag. (2016, November 11). *The 7 Wonders Of The World. World Atlas.* https://www.worldatlas.com/articles/the-7-wonders-of-the-world.html

トップページ. (2021). 大阪大学. https://www.osaka-u.ac.jp/ja

Tokyo Station City. (2022). Tokyostationcity.com. http://www.tokyostationcity.com/en/

Home. (2015, March 2). Home. Maroon 5. https://www.maroon5.com/

Asimov, I. (2022). The Currents of Space (Galactic Empire, #2). In *Goodreads*. https://www.goodreads.com/book/show/7004511-the-currents-of-space